YOUR KNOWLEDGE HAS VALUE

SSH Configuration Interface. Design and Implementation of a "student self-service portal" for accessing to Linux-VMs

Gheorghe Mironica

Bibliographic information published by the German National Library:

The German National Library lists this publication in the National Bibliography; detailed bibliographic data are available on the Internet at http://dnb.dnb.de.

ISBN: 9783346527233
This book is also available as an ebook.

© GRIN Publishing GmbH
Nymphenburger Straße 86
80636 München

Print and binding: Books on Demand GmbH, Norderstedt, Germany
Printed on acid-free paper from responsible sources.

The present work has been carefully prepared. Nevertheless, authors and publishers do not incur liability for the correctness of information, notes, links and advice as well as any printing errors.

GRIN web shop: https://www.grin.com/document/1147465

DEPARTMENT OF INFORMATICS

TECHNISCHE HOCHSCHULE ULM

Bachelor's Thesis in Computer Science

SSH Configuration Interface
Design and Implementation of a "student self-service portal" for accessing to Linux-VMs

Gheorghe Mironica

Acknowledgments

I would like to thank everyone who supported me during the development phase of this project and the thesis as a whole.

- **Prof. Dr. Stefan Traub** for providing a challenging and interesting topic and the constant support during the whole process.

- **Prof. Dr.-Ing. Philipp Graf** for the support provided during the elaboration phase of this thesis.

- **Brecht Baekelandt** for providing a decent guide for advancing the application's architecture and answering all my technical questions.

Abstract

Secure Shell (SSH) is mainly used for managing most of the world's web servers. It creates a secure channel on top of an unsecured network by using the client-server model. The problem arises with the increase in the number of clients that leads to a corresponding increase in the maintenance work for the server administration. This thesis offers an insight into this problem and the solution to it.

The SSH Configuration Interface (SSH CI) is one possible solution to simplify the process. It's a client-server application that provides a simple but intuitive user interface (UI) to the users, so they can upload their public key directly to the server. The server thereon handles the request and, thus, excludes the need of an administration interaction from this process.

Contents

1 Introduction

The SSH protocol uses encryption to secure the connection between a client and a server. It's mainly used to log into a remote machine and execute commands, but there are other useful features available like tunneling and forwarding of Transmission Control Protocol (TCP) ports. An SSH connection supports multiple methods of authentication, the most common being the public key authentication. The advantage of it over a simple password, for example, is security and flexibility. Public key authentication provides a security level that even extremely long passwords can't offer. In a situation where multiple users have access to the same account on the server by using SSH key authentication, it is easy to revoke access to any of them just by deleting their public key from the server. No password has to be shared across the users.

In order to establish an SSH connection, there is a standard procedure. The client must generate an SSH key pair.

"Each SSH key pair includes two keys:

- A public key that is copied to the SSH server(s). Anyone with a copy of the public key can encrypt data that can then only be read by the person who holds the corresponding private key. Once an SSH server receives a public key from a user and considers the key trustworthy, the server marks the key as authorized in its authorized_keys file. Such keys are called authorized keys.

- A private key that remains (only) with the user. The possession of this key is proof of the user's identity. Only a user in possession of a private key that corresponds to the public key at the server will be able to authenticate successfully. The private keys need to be stored and handled carefully, and no copies of the private key should be distributed. The private keys used for user authentication are called identity keys." [12]

Thus, the user is able to log into the server via an SSH client without any password and therefore start a Shell session. An SSH client is a program that handles the establishment of the connection and authentication to the SSH server. The most commonly used clients for Windows and Linux are PuTTY and OpenSSH respectively.

This is a relatively easy and quick process, however, when there are multiple new users to be granted access to the server, the process becomes cumbersome and error-prone. In such circumstances, where a remote virtual machine is shared across multiple users, this becomes a problem that every single organization is going to face as it grows.

The SSH Configuration Interface is an attempt to solve this problem by introducing a cross-platform web-based application that uses the latest web standards and best practices. The purpose of this platform is to partially exclude the system administration from this equation since this is a non critical task that has to be repeated over and over again. The goal is that the user will be able to access a portal via any browser and log in. The user's credentials will be firstly checked against a whitelist, which is a Lightweight Directory Access Protocol (LDAP) directory service. The authorization process follows, it will checks whether the user is enrolled in a specific course. This will limit the user's access to the portal and prevent unauthorized usages. If the previous two steps are completed successfully, the user is redirected to the home page of the application. When he uploads his public key, an account with a limited lifetime will be generated on the SSH server.

As a result, an SSH connection with the server can be started. Thus, on the first sight, the server's administrator's job is reduced to a minimum, that is the application maintenance. Despite the fact that this looks as a relative easy to implement solution, there are pitfalls, obstacles and security issues that have to be addressed. Moreover, as with any other modern distributed application, achieving a loosely coupled and scalable system is a considerable challenge. In this thesis the obstacles and pitfalls of the roadmap for developing such a system will be discussed, as well as the custom solution to them.

2 Technologies

2.1 Multitier Architecture

SSH CI is a three-tier application that implements the client-server model, section 3.2. It is a distributed application that divides tasks to be executed on the client and the server-side. The client-server relationship relies on the request-response communication model. The client sends the request, the server processes it and sends back the response. This architecture is going to be discussed more in detail in section 3.2.

2.1.1 Back-end

Asp.Net Core MVC

The back-end of SSH CI is entirely written in C# 8.0 using the ASP.NET Core MVC framework and Identity framework. C# (pronounced "See Sharp") is a modern, object-oriented, and type-safe programming language. C# has its roots in the C family of languages and will be immediately familiar to C, C++, Java, and JavaScript programmers [4]. ASP.NET Core MVC is a rich framework for building web apps and APIs using the Model-View-Controller (MVC) pattern [3] which is explained in section 3.3.1. It is an open-source, highly testable framework and provides a patterns-based way to build dynamic websites, which helps to achieve a clean separation of concerns. It gives full control over markup and uses the latest web standards. It supports features such as Dependency Injection (section 3.3.4), Model Binding, Routing, and Model Validation that are explained in section 3.3.3 respectively. ASP.NET Core Identity is a framework that refers to the security part of the application. The core features are the middlewares that it offers for supporting the authorization and authentication process. Therefore, an authorization policy can be created and configured to block unauthorized access throughout the whole application. Moreover, it offers functionality for email confirmation, managing the users, roles, claims, tokens, and much more. The Identity framework is typically configured using a Database for the persistence layer.

Nevertheless, in the SSH CI project, it was configured to work along with an LDAP directory service instead. LDAP is discussed in section 3.4.1.

Alternatives

The closest matching alternative worth considering is Java with the Spring MVC framework. Both languages are object-oriented and are a subset of C++. The transition from one to another is very smooth, both including similar features and have similar syntax. Which one suits better, depends on the application's requirements, usage. In a scenario where the best practices and guidelines are followed, both platforms can bring a comparable result.

2.1.2 Front-end

In the MVC pattern, the Views are considered as the presentation layer. ASP.NET Core MVC comes with Razor. It is a markup syntax for integrating server-side code into HTML pages. Therefore, the code is resolved on the server-side, and HTML pages are rendered and then sent to the client. The Razor syntax consists of Razor markup, C#, and HTML [7]. In addition to Razor, SSH CI makes use of jQuery and Bootstrap. jQuery is a fast, small, and feature-rich JavaScript library that makes things like HTML document traversal and manipulation, event handling, animation, and Ajax much simpler with an easy-to-use API that works across a multitude of browsers [10]. Bootstrap is a free and open-source CSS framework directed at responsive, mobile-first front-end web development [14]. It contains CSS design templates for UI components.

2.2 Persistence Layer

In a typical three-tier application, the persistence layer is covered by a relational or non-relational database management system (DBMS). However, in the case of SSH CI, that is handled by an LDAP directory service. The relation between LDAP and a directory service is similar to Structured Query Language (SQL) and a relational database. LDAP protocol and directory services are explained more in detail in section 3.4.2.

2.2.1 Novell's Library for LDAP

ASP.NET Core does not provide any library for accessing an LDAP directory by default. For the older ASP.NET framework, a built-in library [8] was available for accessing Microsoft Active Directory. The newer framework is a complete rewrite of the old one, hence, it became cross-platform. Thus, the existing library got obsolete and unavailable since it was designed for the Windows operating system (OS). However, the solution came from a third-party library. The most suitable one is Novell's LDAP library [13]. It works with any LDAP-compatible directory service.

2.3 NLog Framework

Logging errors in an application server is important. An application log is simply a file that contains specific information. It can be used for data collection, for user experience (UX) improvement or simply for issues investigation like in SSH CI. In ASP.NET Core there is no built in support for file or database logging. A viable solution is NLog, a third-party framework. Logging with NLog is discussed in section 4.3.

2.4 Security Layer

The security layer in SSH CI consists mainly of Google's reCaptcha service [11] and other security controls. ReCaptcha is a CAPTCHA system (section 5.1). It helps web hosts to detect bots and distinguish between human and automated interaction with the website. Moreover, additional security measures were taken against Brute-force and Open Redirect attacks (section 5.2).

2.5 Tools

The SSH CI is fully developed, tested, and debugged with Microsoft Visual Studio integrated development environment (IDE). It is an indispensable IDE for C# development that is equipped with all the C# environment-related tools like IntelliSense, database schema designer, version control system, and many others. IntelliSense is an intelligent code completion embedded tool that speeds up the development process and reduces common typos and mistakes. The application is versioned and tracked with Git and hosted on GitHub. Finally, the testing phase of the development cycle was arranged on the target operating system, which is Linux.

The operating system was emulated by using Oracle VM VirtualBox. It is a tool that allows users to emulate a physical computer and provides the functionality of it.

3 Architecture

3.1 User Activity

The SSH CI is a user friendly and intuitive application. The interaction between the user and the application is estimated to be around 2 to 3 minutes. Firstly, the user has to access the web application with any web-browser. The server checks if any authentication cookie has been provided in the HTTP request header. The cookie authentication is described more in detail in section 3.4.3. If no cookie was found, that means the user is not logged in, and he will be automatically redirected to the login page where he can authenticate. The submitted request is analyzed by an external CAPTCHA system, thereafter, the credentials are validated by the server. If the previous two steps were completed successfully, the user is redirected to the home page where he can manipulate his private key. Whenever the user performs any actions regarding his key, specific scripts will be launched that will manipulate the key. On each action, his behavior is scanned by the CAPTCHA system. Suspicious actions may lead the user to be logged out of the system. The graphical illustration of the whole process can be observed in fig. 3.1.

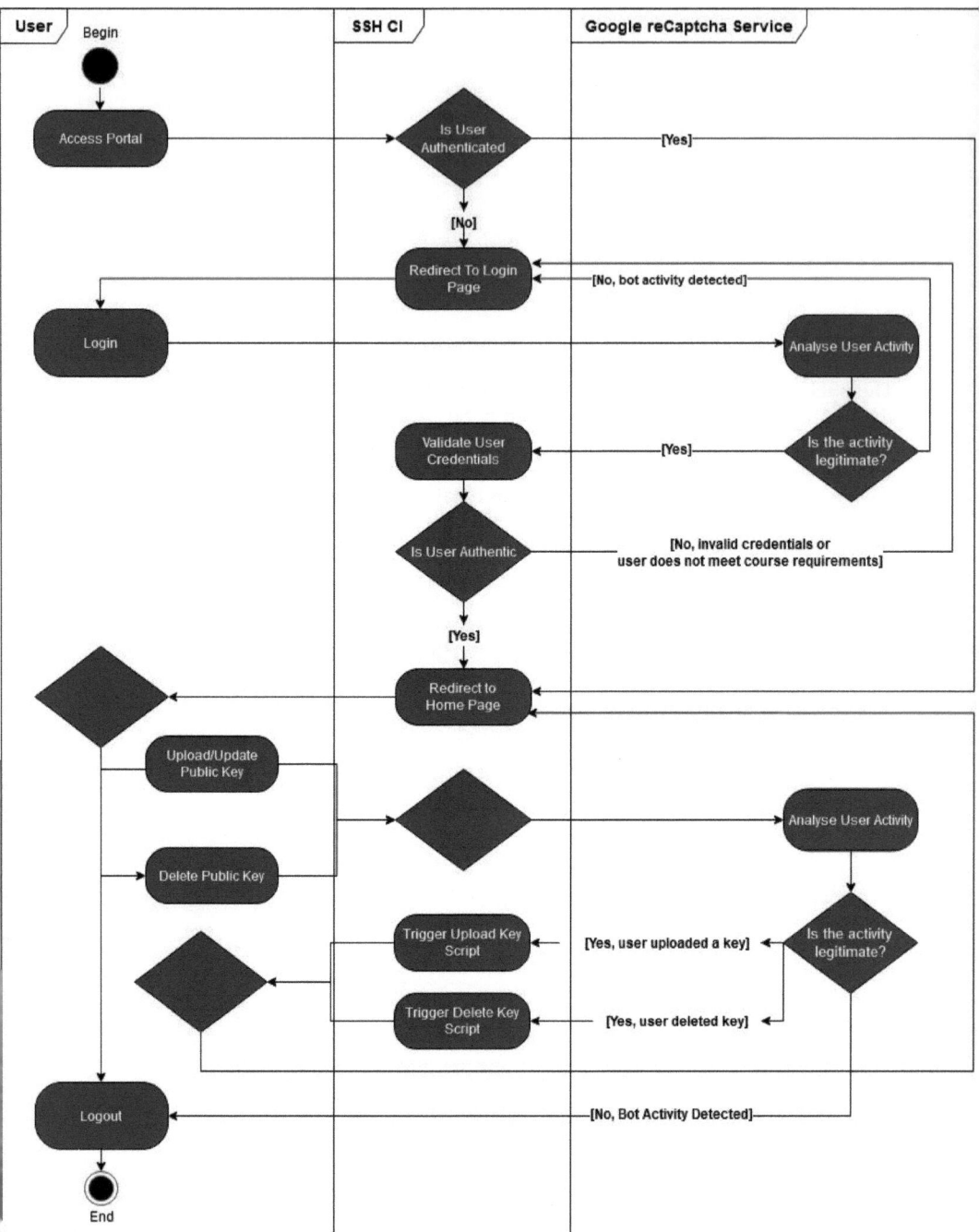

Figure 3.1: Interaction between the system and the user - activity diagram

3.2 Physical Deployment Model

The SSH CI is a three-tier application that implements the client-server model. The system is split between the presentation tier, business logic tier, and the data tier as can be seen in fig. 3.2.

- The business logic tier is where the logic of the application is implemented. It is located on the application server side. It is responsible for all the decision making, for rendering the views for the presentation layer, and for interacting with the data layer.

- The data tier is where all the user's data is stored. In the SSH CI scenario, the LDAP directory stores the data. The data tier communicates only with the business logic layer via TCP/IP protocol on port 636, which is the default port of any directory service for Transport Layer Security (TLS) connections.

- The presentation tier is the front-end layer. It consists mainly of the UI. The user interface is accessible through a web browser and it acts as a mediator between the end-user and the business layer of the application. The presentation layer logic, is distributed across the client and the server. On the client side the Javascript code is running in the web browser, on the server-side, the Razor markup, which is integrated in the HTML pages.

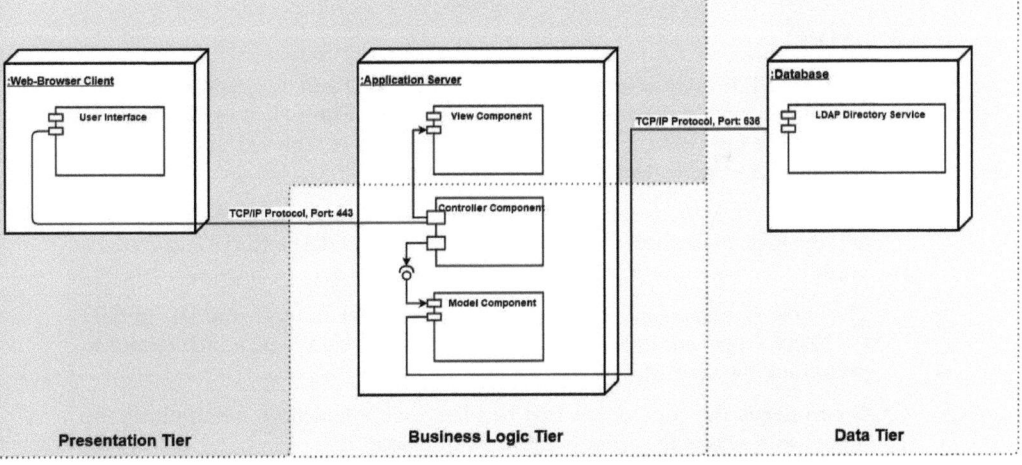

Figure 3.2: SSH CI - deployment diagram

As described previously, SSH CI implements the client-server model. The client is the end user's browser and the server, the web server. The communication between the two is of type request-response. The exchanged messages are called Hypertext

Transfer Protocol (HTTP) messages and are sent over TCP/IP protocol. As HTTP is a stateless protocol, each request-response is isolated from each other. In the context of a protocol, stateless means that the server is not required to track the state over multiple requests and does not retain any information. In a non-persistent connection, the client always requests, and the server responds.

- An HTTP request consists mainly of the request line, the header, and the message body. The header contains the request line that specifies the HTTP method, the path, and the protocol. The method indicates what kind of action should be done on the server, the path is generally the desired part of the Uniform Resource Locator (URL) that comes after the domain. Finally, the protocol denotes the HTTP version.

- An HTTP response has at the basis the same components as the request except there is a response line instead of a request line. The response line contains the protocol and status code. In the response header, the server passes additional information about the response. Lastly, the response body can contain a HTML page, Javascript Object Notation (JSON) or an Extensible Markup Language (XML) formatted result.

3.3 Application Structure

3.3.1 MVC

In SSH CI, the MVC architectural pattern is implemented and it separates the application into three main components: Models, Views, and Controllers as illustrated in fig. 3.3. By using this pattern, the separation of concerns is achieved. It ensures that the application is scalable, testable and loosely coupled.

- The model in MVC is the set of classes that encapsulates the business object and the logic to perform the create, read, update, and delete (CRUD) operations on it.

- The view is responsible for presenting the model through the UI. In SSH CI, Razor views are used and they combine minimum logic which relates to presenting the content.

- Controller is the component that handles user interaction, manipulates the model, and selects the appropriate view to render it.

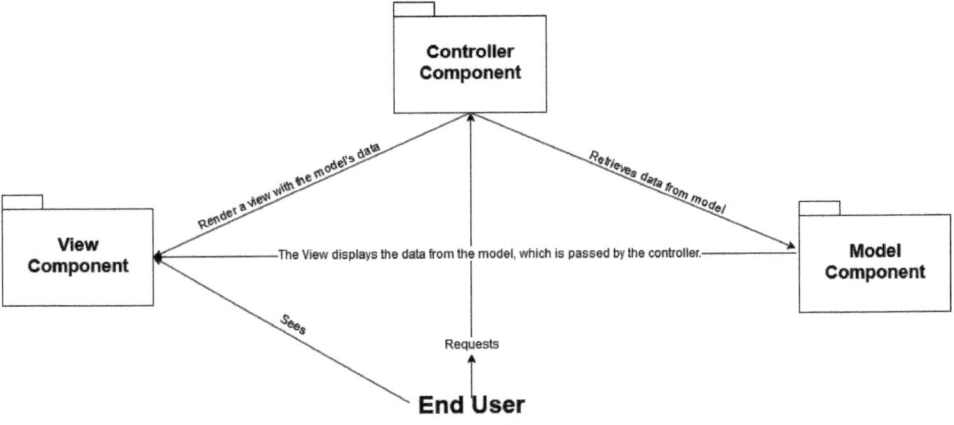

Figure 3.3: MVC architecture pattern

3.3.2 Programming Model

When an HTTP request comes in, the framework assigns one thread from the thread pool to the request. The thread pool itself is managed by the framework. Nevertheless, the way the threads are used depends on the implemented programming model. In the case of synchronous implementation, the assigned tasks will block the thread. The next incoming requests are going to be queued and wait for the thread to free up, which may lead to the server responding with HTTP Error 503 status code (Service unavailable). The programming model implemented in SSH CI is Asynchronous. Whenever a request reaches the server, the framework assigns a thread to the request as well. However, all the input/output (IO) operations will be performed asynchronously. This returns the thread to the thread pool until the IO operation returns, thus, other requests can be served in the meantime. An IO operation can be performed on a file, database, or a web API. The asynchronous programming model allows a small number of threads to handle a much larger number of requests. Subsequently, the primary benefit of asynchronous code is scalability.

3.3.3 Request Lifecycle

As discussed earlier, SSH CI is stateless since it's a server-side web application that uses HTTP protocol for communication. Each HTTP request has its own lifecycle. As shown in fig. 3.4, the lifecycle consists of following states:

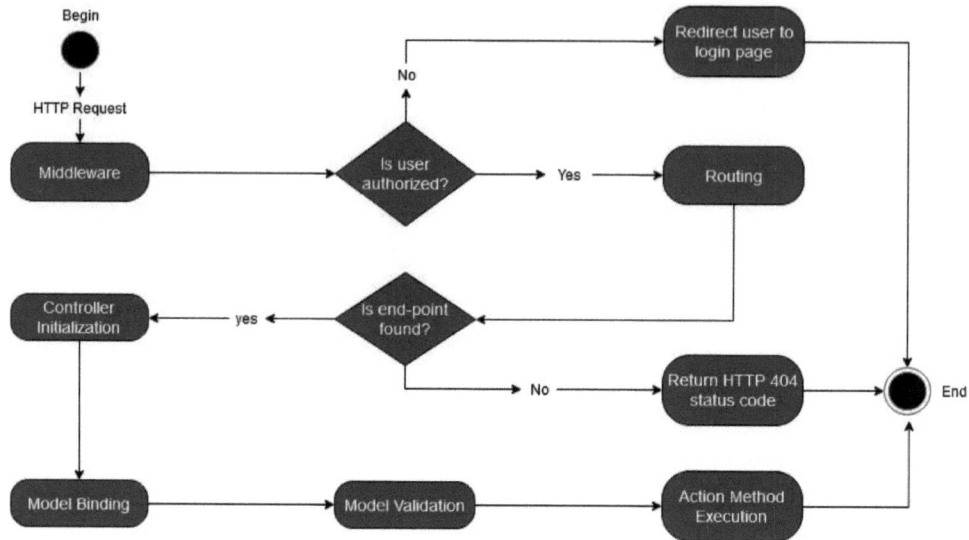

Figure 3.4: SSH CI application lifecycle - activity diagram.

- **The Middleware** component forms the basic building block of the application's HTTP pipeline [1]. There might be several middlewares that are executed sequentially. Once the request enters the pipeline, the first middleware may simply pass the request to the next one, process the request then pass it to the next one or it may just handle it and short-circuit the pipeline. In SSH CI there are several middlewares integrated like authorization and authentication. It is in their responsibility to determine whether the user is authenticated and has access to the requested resource. Eventually, the request is either forwarded to the next state or handled and then short-circuited as illustrated in fig. 3.4.

- **Routing** is used for handling the MVC URLs. It is responsible for mapping an incoming request to Controllers and endpoints. Endpoints are the action methods that are the application's units of executable request-handling code. The default routing configuration looks as in fig. 3.5.

Figure 3.5: Default routing configuration

- **Controller Initialization**, as the name suggests, is the stage of the application's lifecycle when the controller is initialized. The Controller is initialized by the "MvcMiddleware", the constructor is called and the required dependencies are injected from the DI container. Finally, the appropriate action method is executed.

- **Model Binding** maps the incoming HTTP request to the action method's parameters. Using the acquired data from the request, it instantiates an object and passes it as an argument to the action method. The model binder searches for the following values in the request's form data, routing variables or in the query string data. Each of these sources are examined sequentially until a matching argument value is found. As an example, an HTTP GET request to this URL:

```
https://localhost:5000/sample/index?userId=randomGuid&token=authenticToken
```

will fire up the following controller and the "Index" action method will be invoked. The "userId", and "token" input parameters will be retrieved from the query string of the HTTP request.

```
public class SampleController : Controller
{
    // GET sample/index?userId=example&token=example
    [HttpGet]
    public async Task<IActionResult> Index(string userId, string token)
    {
        // action method logic
        // ...
        return View();
    }
}
```

Code Snippet 3.1: Example of a basic controller, with an action method.

- **Model Validation**, as the name implies, validates the incoming arguments for the action method. This process occurs after model binding and detects errors related to the model state. The validation is done automatically, but the rules must be predefined in the model, as shown in the following code snippet from SSH CI:

```
public class LoginViewModel
{
    [Required]
    [Display(Name = "Username")]
    public string UserName { get; set; }

    [Required]
    [DataType(DataType.Password)]
    public string Password { get; set; }

    [Required]
    public string Token { get; set; }

    [Display(Name = "Remember me")]
    public bool RememberMe { get; set; }
}
```

Code Snippet 3.2: Model Validation - *LoginViewModel.cs*

```
public class AccountController : Controller
{
    [HttpPost]
    public async Task<IActionResult> Login(LoginViewModel model, string
        returnUrl)
    {
        // Controller logic
        if (!ModelState.IsValid)
        {
            return View(model);
        }
        // Controller logic continued...
        return View();
    }
}
```

Code Snippet 3.3: Model Validation - *AccountController.cs*

In Code Snippet 3.2 and Code Snippet 3.3 example, the model validation middleware will validate the action method's incoming arguments according to the model's rules, which are the validation attributes and the data types. There are plenty of other validation attributes available for validating email addresses, regular expressions, phone numbers, URLs and others. When the model validation fails, an automatic HTTP response with 400 status code is returned containing the auto-generated error messages rendered in the initial view, as shown in fig. 3.6 below.

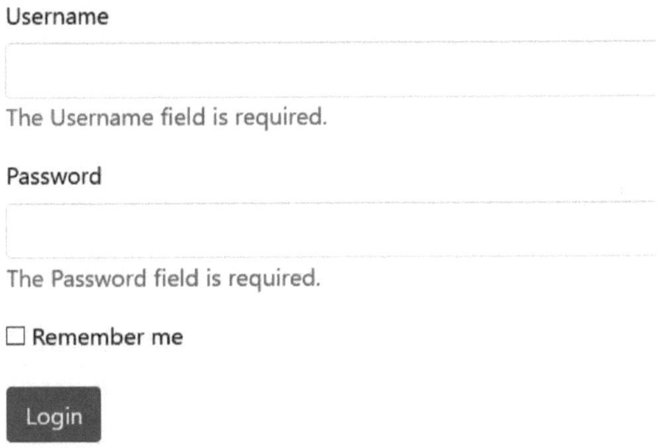

Username

The Username field is required.

Password

The Password field is required.

☐ Remember me

Login

Figure 3.6: Model validation example

- **The Action Method Execution** is the final stage where the implemented logic for handling the user's interactions is executed. It is the action method's responsibility to generate a response to an incoming HTTP request. It can return any object that implements the "IActionResult" interface from the "AspNetCore.Mvc" namespace. Depending on the result of the action method, a response can be a rendered view, JSON or XML format response or redirection to another URL. In case of a JSON or XML format response, the action method can return a simple Plain Old CLR Object (POCO). The runtime eventually automatically serializes the object into a JSON or XML and returns it.

3.3.4 Dependency Injection

SSH CI heavily relies on Dependency Injection. ASP.NET Core has built-in support for DI which is a software design pattern used for achieving Inversion of Control (IoC) between classes and their dependencies. It is an imperative technique for building modern, loosely coupled applications. The end applications are more unit-testable, modular, and maintainable as result. In a scenario similar as in fig. 3.7, class A is directly dependent on Class B. This might be a problem when trying to replace B with a different implementation, class A must be modified. In a large project with multiple classes depending on B, the code becomes strewed across the application. This kind of implementation significantly complicates the unit testing. Class B has to be involved in the unit testing of class A which breaks the unit testing principles.

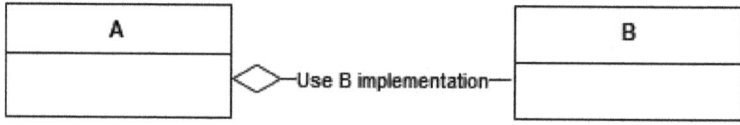

Figure 3.7: Direct Dependency - class diagram

Nevertheless, DI addresses this problem by using an interface to abstract away the dependency implementation as demonstrated with an example from SSH CI, fig. 3.8. Registration of the dependency is done in the service container provided by the framework. In ASP.NET Core they are registered in the application's "Startup" class, in the "ConfigureServices" method, however, in SSH CI the container is distributed across several "Installer" classes for establishing a more structured service registration mechanism. Therefore, a more maintainable application is achieved. This approach will be discussed in section 3.3.5. As a result, it's easy to change the implementation that "AccountController" uses without modifying the controller.

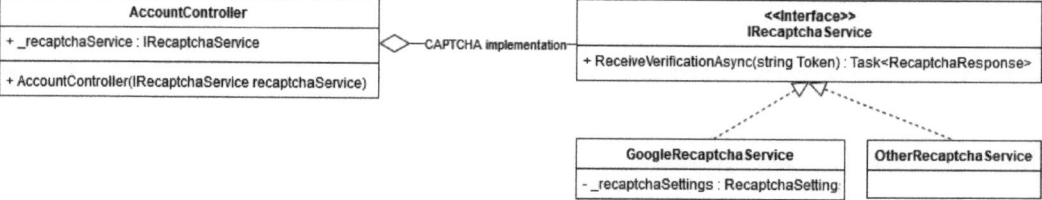

Figure 3.8: Inversion of control - class diagram

In the scenario as illustrated in fig. 3.8, it's easy to configure the implementation of the "IRecaptchaService" interface that the "AccountController" uses. The dependency is registered in the application's Startup class with the "ConfigureServices" method as following:

```csharp
public class Startup
{
    public Startup(IConfiguration configuration)
    {
            Configuration = configuration;
    }

    public IConfiguration Configuration { get; }

    // This method gets called by the runtime. It is used to add services to the DI
        container.
    public void ConfigureServices(IServiceCollection services)
    {
        services.AddTransient<IRecaptchaService, GoogleRecaptchaService>();
        // ...
    }
    // ...
}
```

Code Snippet 3.4: Startup class - *Startup.cs*

The services can be registered with three kinds of lifetime:

- Singleton - The service is instantiated the first time it is requested, and the instance is shared across requests.

- Transient - The service is created each time it is requested from the service container. It is disposed at the end of the request.

- Scoped - The service is instantiated for every client request, and then disposed.

3.3.5 Improved Service Registration Mechanism

The provided solution by the ASP.NET Core regarding the service registration is basic. It works perfectly fine in a small project. However, as the solution grows, the "ConfigureServices" method from the "Startup" class becomes overwhelmed with registered services that are unassociated to each other. Maintaining and tracking these services with this approach is challenging and time consuming. The solution to this problem that is implemented in SSH CI looks as illustrated in fig. 3.9.

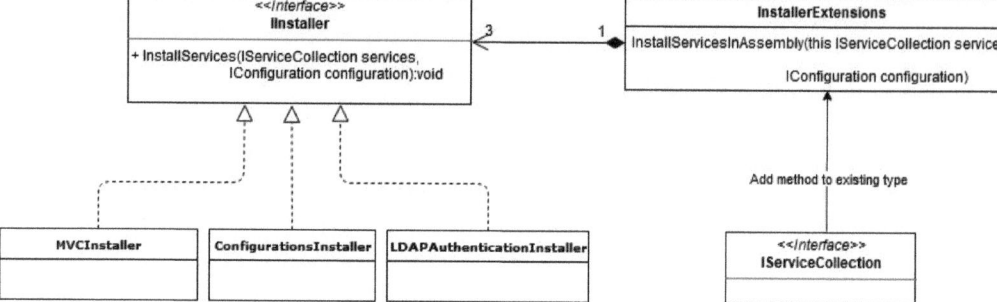

Figure 3.9: Improved service registration - class diagram

The "MVCInstaller", "LDAPAuthenticationInstaller" and the "ConfigurationsIn-staller" classes implement the "InstallServices" method from the "IInstaller" interface with the DI container as an input parameter (IServiceCollection interface). Inside the "InstallServices" method of these classes the services related to the framework functionality, LDAP directory, and application configurations respectively, are registered in the DI container. Hence, all the related services are aggregated and containerized in different "Installer" classes. The "InstallerExtensions" is a static class containing the "InstallServicesInAssembly" extension method. Extension methods in C# are meant for appending methods to existing types without deriving or modifying the original type. As a result, extension methods are called as if they were instance methods. Eventually, there is no observable difference between calling an extension method or a method defined in a type. Inside this method all classes that implement the "IInstaller" interface are enumerated in a list, instantiated, and the "InstallServices" method is called for each instance.

This mechanism is triggered by the "ConfigureServices" method from "Startup" class, which is called by the runtime. When the "InstallServicesInAssembly" method is called from the DI container instance, all the configured services will be containerized as demonstrated in Code Snippet 3.5.

```
public class Startup
{
    public Startup(IConfiguration configuration)
    {
        Configuration = configuration;
    }

    public IConfiguration Configuration { get; }

    // This method gets called by the runtime. It is used to add services to the DI
        container.
    public void ConfigureServices(IServiceCollection services)
    {
        // The extension method
        services.InstallServicesInAssembly(Configuration);
    }
    // ...
}
```

Code Snippet 3.5: Startup class - *Startup.cs*

As a result, the "Startup" class is kept clean. As the project grows, more "Installer" classes can be easily added for groups of related services, therefore the code is more readable and the application is maintainable.

3.4 Data Access

3.4.1 Directory Service

"A directory is similar to a database, but typically contains more descriptive, attribute-based data; that is, data read more often than it is written. Also, a directory contains data that is concise and strictly relevant to an entry. By contrast, a database contains large amounts of data for each entry that may, or may not, be directly relevant to the entry. For this reason, a directory does not usually implement the transaction or roll-back schemes that regular databases require. If they are permitted at all, directory updates are typically simple all-or-nothing changes. Directories are tuned to respond quickly to high-volume lookup or search operations." [5]

The LDAP on the other hand, is an application layer protocol that uses port 389 for unsecure and 636 for secure connection via TCP. "LDAP, the Lightweight Directory Access Protocol, is a mature, flexible, and well supported standards-based mechanism for interacting with directory servers. It's often used for authentication and storing information about users, groups, and applications, but an LDAP directory server is a fairly general-purpose data store and can be used in a wide variety of applications." [15]

In SSH CI the authentication is implemented using a directory service. The advantages of this approach are discussed in section 3.4.2 as well as the implementation details, section 4.4.

3.4.2 Directory Service compared to DBMS

Both databases and directories can store data. The key difference is that directories are optimized for read rather then write operations. They offer greater performance than DBMS. The write operations on the other hand are worse in terms of performance. Nevertheless, in SSH CI, the public keys are stored on the application server's storage. The only data that is being stored in a datastore is the user's data (username, email, password, semester, subjects, etc). In the current use case, only read operations are relevant, which are required for authentication and authorization. Thus, the directory service is more feasible for this scenario.

3.4.3 Authentication and Authorization

As mentioned earlier, the default setup for the Identity Framework is working along with Entity Framework which uses a database for storing the user's credentials, roles, and claims. The Identity Framework is a key technology for implementing the authorization and authentication components in a C# application. In SSH CI, the LDAP directory service replaces the usual DBMS. Such an implementation requires overriding the behavior of some framework's services. A very decent guide on how to harmonize the Identity Framework with Novell's library for accessing an LDAP directory service came from Brecht Baekelandt's blog [2]. This implementation will be analyzed in section 4.4. The main two services of this framework are the "UserManager", and the "SignInManager". The "UserManager" service is used to perform CRUD operations on a user whereas "SignInManager" is used to handle user's credentials, and authenticate the user. When the user tries to login, the "SignInManager" services check's the credentials against the LDAP directory service. Thereafter, it checks whether the user is enrolled is some specific courses.

If the previous two conditions are met, a persistent or a session cookie is generated by the server and stored in user's browser. The persistent cookie is generated if the user clicks the "Remember Me" checkbox on the login page, as previously illustrated in fig. 3.6, otherwise the server signs a simple session cookie which expires when the web-browser is closed. This cookie is passed along with each request, thus, the server recognizes the user. "An HTTP cookie (web cookie, browser cookie) is a small piece of data that a server sends to the user's web browser. The browser may store it and send it back with later requests to the same server. Typically, it's used to tell if two requests came from the same browser — keeping a user logged-in, for example. It remembers stateful information for the stateless HTTP protocol." [9]

3.5 Configurations

The SSH CI application is configured using the default configuration provider which is the "appsettings.json" file. It stores data as key-value pairs. Alternative providers can be the environment variables, and the command-line arguments as well as custom providers. In SSH CI, various services can be configured such as:

- User's public key and account lifetime
- Portal access restrictions (list of code names of the subjects that a user must be enrolled in for accessing the platform. At least one match is required)
- LDAP Directory settings
- Google ReCaptcha keys

The conventional way of accessing them is by binding them to typed classes, and adding them to the DI service container using Options Pattern.

"The options pattern uses classes to provide strongly typed access to groups of related settings. When configuration settings are isolated by scenario into separate classes, the app adheres to two important software engineering principles:

- The Interface Segregation Principle (ISP) or Encapsulation: Scenarios (classes) that depend on configuration settings depend only on the configuration settings that they use.
- Separation of Concerns: Settings for different parts of the app aren't dependent or coupled to one another.[6]

As an example can be considered the following excerpts from SSH CI. In this demo, the mandated subject code names are configured.

```
"Courses": {
    "CourseNames": [
        "043048101010", // operating systems code name
        "043086961000" // distributed systems code name
    ]
},
```

Code Snippet 3.6: Configuration provider - *appsettings.json*

```
public class AllowedCourses
{
    public List<String> CourseNames { get; set; }
}
```

Code Snippet 3.7: Options class for binding settings - *AllowedCourses.cs*

```
// ...
services.Configure<AllowedCourses>(configuration.GetSection("Courses"));
// ...
```

Code Snippet 3.8: Registering a service in an installer class - *ConfigurationInstaller.cs*

The "AllowedCourses" class containing the settings from the "appsettings.json" are now registered in the container class with the Singleton lifetime using the "Configure" method of the DI container interface.

4 Implementation

4.1 Hosting Environment

The SSH CI is configured to operate differently depending on the hosting environment. There are two main hosting environments, development and production. The environment can be configured from the "launchSettings.json" file for the local development machine and with environment variables for the target machine. When running the application from the command line, the default hosting environment is production, unless configured otherwise by setting an environment variable as in the example below:

```
$ export ASPNETCORE_ENVIRONMENT="Development"
```

Code Snippet 4.1: Setting an environment variable in shell.

The goal of having different environments is for enabling features in the development environment which are not going to be exposed in production, and being able to configure them without modifying the code. As an example, in SSH CI the developer exception page is exposed only in the development environment which will be explained in section 4.2.

4.2 Error Handling

A global exception handler can strengthen the applications' error handling logic. The error states have to be reported to the client by leveraging an appropriate view. Despite that, the detailed information about the error should never be displayed to the users in a production environment. In SSH CI, different views will be returned to the user depending on the error while the exceptions are logged to files sorted by date. Logging is explained in section 4.3. However, when the application is in a development environment, SSH CI is configured to return a developer exception page containing the error and the stack trace. Thus, the developer will observe the error immediately without having to parse the log files.

In SSH CI, the error handling mechanism consists of few components and configurations.

- The error handling middleware
- Error controller
- Error state views

The following excerpt is an example from SSH CI:

```
public void Configure(IApplicationBuilder app, IWebHostEnvironment env)
{
    if (env.IsDevelopment())
    {
        app.UseDeveloperExceptionPage();
    }
    else
    {
        app.UseStatusCodePagesWithRedirects("/Error/{0}");
        app.UseExceptionHandler("/Error");
        app.UseHsts();
    }
    // ...
}
```

Code Snippet 4.2: Configuration method - *Startup.cs*

The preceding code is disabling the developer exception page when the application is running in a production or staging environment. The errors will be caught by the Exception Handler middleware and the request will be redirected to the error handling controller. Another middleware used here is "UseStatusCodePagesWithRedirects". Whenever the user navigates to an nonexistent path of the application, by default the server responds with a simple text response "Status Code: 404; Not Found". This middleware intercepts the non-successful requests and redirects them to the specified controller.

```
public class ErrorController : Controller
{
    // ...

    [Route("Error/{statusCode}")]
    public async Task<IActionResult> HttpStatusCodeHandler(int statusCode)
    {
        var statusCodeResult = HttpContext.Features.Get<IStatusCodeReExecuteFeature>();

        switch (statusCode)
        {
            case 404:
            ViewBag.ErrorMessage = "Sorry, the resource you requested could not be
                found";
            break;
        }

        return View("NotFound");
    }

    [Route("Error")]
    [AllowAnonymous]
    public async Task<IActionResult> Error()
    {
        var exceptionDetails =
            HttpContext.Features.Get<IExceptionHandlerPathFeature>();
        // log the exception to file
        return View("Error");
    }
}
```

Code Snippet 4.3: Error controller - *ErrorController.cs*

The above block of code is the error handling controller. After the middleware catches any unhandled exceptions, it redirects them to this controller. In this controller, there are two action methods. The first one, "HttpStatusCodeHandler" is decorated with the Route attribute. Attribute routing maps actions directly to URL templates. This method is configured to accepts redirected requests from the middleware with status codes, particularly HTTP 404. After such a request is processed, a custom page is returned to the user. The second action method is triggered only when an internal server error occurs. When the "UseExceptionHandler" middleware will handle an error, it will route it to the "Error" action method. In SSH CI, the error is logged. Thereafter a custom error message can be passed to the view through a ViewBag.

Finally, the view can be rendered and returned to the user. ViewBag is used to pass a small amount of data to the view as dynamic properties.

```
@ if(ViewBag.ErrorTitle == null)
{
    <h3>
        An error occured while processing the request.
        The support team is notified and we are working on the fix.
    </h3>
}
else
{
    <h1 class="text-danger">@ ViewBag.ErrorTitle</h1>
    <h6 class="text-danger">@ ViewBag.ErrorMessage</h6>
}
```

Code Snippet 4.4: Error state view - *Error.cshtml*

The last bits of code represented above are from the Error View. If no information has been passed to the view through view bags, a default message is rendered to the user.

4.3 Logging

For an application server, logging is a decisive feature for application maintenance, investigating issues, and debugging. In SSH CI, all the exceptions and server-side errors are logged to files and sorted by date. As mentioned earlier, ASP.NET Core has no built-in support for file logging, therefore Nlog framework was used. When enabling logging with Nlog, by default, it will attempt to load the configurations from "nlog.config", however, a custom configuration provider was created for this purpose, which is "Nlog.json", as JSON files are more readable than XML since they contain less metadata. In this configuration file, the path for the logs can be specified. Depending on the operating system, it has to be manually configured. There are features configured for appending the date to the log file and specifying the action method and the controller where the error occurred.

In order to enable logging with Nlog, the package was installed, then added to the dependencies in the applications ".csproj" file. In addition to the default logging providers, Nlog was added using the extension method "AddNLog" in the "Program" class's "CreateHostBuilder" method. Replacing or disabling NLog is as easy as removing the line with the emphasized code.

```
public static IHostBuilder CreateHostBuilder(string[] args) =>
    Host.CreateDefaultBuilder(args)
    // ...
    ConfigureLogging((hostingContext, logging) =>
    {
        logging.AddConfiguration(hostingContext.Configuration.GetSection("Logging"));
        logging.AddConsole();
        logging.AddDebug();
        logging.AddEventSourceLogger();
        // Enable NLog as a Logging Provider
        logging.AddNLog();
    })
    // ...
```

The following example is a section from the Nlog configuration file.

```
"targets": {
    "mylogs": {
      "type": "File",
      "fileName": "Logs\\errors-${shortdate}.log",
      "layout":
          "${longdate}|${event-properties:item=EventId_Id}|${uppercase:${level}}|$
          {logger}|${message} ${exception:format=tostring}|url:
          ${aspnet-request-url}|  action: ${aspnet-mvc-action}"
    }
},
```

Code Snippet 4.5: *NLog.json* file

As can be seen, there are a various things that can be configured for structuring the logging such as including the URL and the action method that triggered the error, the timestamp, and many others.

4.4 Identity Framework with LDAP

A directory server is a type of database that stores the information as trees of entries. An LDAP entry contains a collection of information about an entity. An entity consists mainly of few components:

- A distinguished name (DN) uniquely identifies an entry and it's position in the tree. The DN of an entry is somewhat similar to a file's path in the file system.

- Attributes stores the data of an entry, and they have an attribute type. Attribute types specify the attribute's syntax which indicates what type of data can be stored (e.g. UUID, Boolean, etc.).

- Object classes are elements that specify a collection of attribute types related to an entity. Object classes may indicate what kind of information is stored about the entity (e.g. personal data of an individual, service information, etc.).

The Code Snippet 4.6, is an example of how to authenticate a user with a password and retrieve his data from a directory service with LDAP. The target directory service has a structure similar to the one illustrated in fig. 4.1.

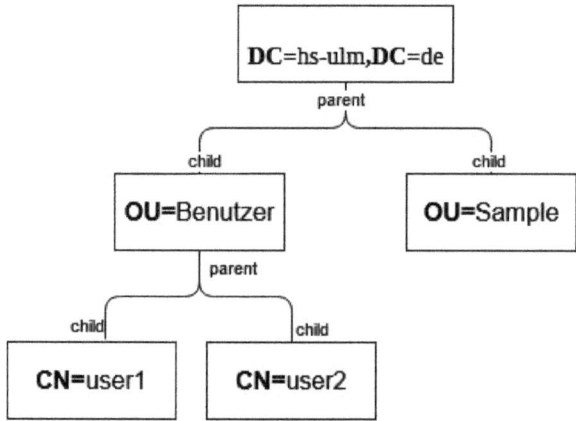

Figure 4.1: Directory Service tree representation

```
$ ldapsearch -D "cn=username,ou=Benutzer,dc=hs-ulm,dc=de" -W -h
  rz-peter.hs-ulm.de -b "ou=Benutzer,dc=hs-ulm,dc=de" -s sub
  'mail=user@mail.hs-ulm.de'
```

Code Snippet 4.6: Querying using LDAP search

The preceding statement is read from right (root) to left (leaf) and can be decomposed as following:

- **The search filter** comes first, that is "mail=user@email.hs-ulm.de". In this case an entry with this email will be searched.

- **-s** sub is the search scope, and sub is for recursive searching down the tree.

- **-b** specifies the search base.

- **-h** indicates the LDAP url.

- **-W** prompts for the user's password.

- **-D** is used for binding operations.

Bind operations are used to authenticate users. In SSH CI it's required for identifying a person for further actions. Such operation is replicated in SSH CI with the Novell's LDAP library. The implementation is very similar to the one from Brecht's guide, as already mentioned.

The first step was configuring the directory server's domain and port in the "appsettings.json" file and binding it to a type (LdapSettings) with Options Pattern as in the following block:

```
"LdapSettings": {
    "ServerName": "rz-peter.hs-ulm.de",
    "ServerPort": 636,
    "UseSSL": true,
    "SearchBase": "OU=Benutzer,DC=hs-ulm,DC=de",
    "ContainerName": "CN=Users,DC=hs-ulm,DC=de",
    "DomainName": "hs-ulm.de",
    "DomainDistinguishedName": "DC=hs-ulm,DC=de"
}
```

Code Snippet 4.7: Directory service settings - *appsettings.json*

```
public class LdapSettings
{
    public string ServerName { get; set; }
    public int ServerPort { get; set; }
    public bool UseSSL { get; set; }
    public string SearchBase { get; set; }
    public string ContainerName { get; set; }
    public string DomainName { get; set; }
    public string DomainDistinguishedName { get; set; }
}
```

Code Snippet 4.8: The Ldap Settings - *LdapSettings.cs*

In the above's settings, the directory's domain, and the port is configured. In order to use LDAP over TLS, port 636 is used.

The second step is creating a model class, for storing the entity data retrieved the directory service. After a successful binding to the directory server, the user's data will be mapped to such an object:

```
public class THUMember : IdentityUser, ILdapEntry
{
    public string ObjectSid { get; set; }
    public string ObjectGuid { get; set; }
    public string ObjectCategory { get; set; }
    public string ObjectClass { get; set; }
    public string Name { get; set; }
    public string CommonName { get; set; }
    public string DistinguishedName { get; set; }
    public string DisplayName { get; set; }
    public List<string> MemberOf { get; set; }
}
```

Code Snippet 4.9: The user data model - *THUMember.cs*

The "THUMember" type extends "IdentityUser" and "IldapEntry" interface. The "IdentityUser" class is the base class that contains information about users registered in the application. This is required for being able to make use of "UserManager", and "SignInManager" services from Identity Framework.

The next step is creating a service that will bind to the directory and retrieve the user's data.

```
public interface ILdapService
{
    THUMember GetUserByUserName(string userName, string password);
}
```

Code Snippet 4.10: The interface for Ldap Service - *ILdapService.cs*

```
public class LdapService : ILdapService
{
    public LdapService(IOptions<LdapSettings> ldapSettings);
    private ILdapConnection GetConnection(string userName, string password);
    public THUMember GetUserByUserName(string userName, string password);
    private THUMember CreateUserFromAttributes(string dN, LdapAttributeSet
        attributeSet);
}
```

Code Snippet 4.11: The implementation class signature - *LdapService.cs*

The function and the sequence of execution of these methods are explained later. This is all that is needed to bind to an LDAP directory, authenticate a user, and retrieve his data. However, one last step is required for using this service in the Identity Framework.

Two classes are created that extend "UserManager and "SignInManager". The "IldapService" will be injected in the "UserManager" service. In comparison with the default "UserManager" service, the extended version will make use of the "LdapService" to authenticate and retrieve user's data.

```
public class LdapUserManager : UserManager<THUMember>
{
      private readonly ILdapService ldapService;

    // constructor, injecting ldapService with DI

      public Task<THUMember> FindByNameAsync(string userName, string password)
      {
          return Task.FromResult(this.ldapService.GetUserByUserName(userName,
              password));
      }

    // ...
}
```

Code Snippet 4.12: *LdapUserManager.cs*

```
public class LdapSignInManager : SignInManager<THUMember>
{
    private readonly IOptions<AllowedCourses> coursesOptions;
    private readonly LdapUserManager ldapUserManager;

    // constructor, injecting required services with DI

    public override async Task<SignInResult> PasswordSignInAsync(string userName,
        string password, bool rememberMe, bool lockOutOnFailure)
    {
        var user = await ldapUserManager.FindByNameAsync(userName , password);
        if (user == null)
        {
            return SignInResult.Failed;
        }

        var validUser = false;
        if (coursesOptions.Value.CourseNames != null)
        {
            foreach (var course in coursesOptions.Value.CourseNames)
            {
                if (user.MemberOf.FirstOrDefault(s => s.Contains(course)) != null)
                validUser = true;
            }
            if (!validUser)
            {
                return SignInResult.NotAllowed;
            }
        }
        return await this.PasswordSignInAsync(user, password, rememberMe,
            lockOutOnFailure);
    }
}
```

Code Snippet 4.13: *LdapSignInManager.cs*

The final step is registering the overridden services in the DI container and implementing the controller logic.

```csharp
public void InstallServices(IServiceCollection services, IConfiguration configuration)
{
    services.Configure<LdapSettings>(configuration.GetSection("LdapSettings"));
    services.AddDbContext<DataContext>(options => options
        .UseInMemoryDatabase("testdb"));
    services.AddIdentity<THUMember, IdentityRole>()
        .AddUserManager<LdapUserManager>()
        .AddSignInManager<LdapSignInManager>()
        .AddEntityFrameworkStores<DataContext>()
        .AddDefaultTokenProviders();
}
```

Code Snippet 4.14: InstallServices method - *LdapAuthenticationInstaller.cs*

```csharp
[AllowAnonymous]
[HttpPost]
public async Task<IActionResult> Login(LoginViewModel model, string returnUrl)
{
    // Google Recaptcha Verification ...
    // Model state verification ...

    var result = await signInManager.PasswordSignInAsync(model.UserName,
        model.Password,    model.RememberMe, false);

    if (result.Succeeded)
    {
        // ...
        return RedirectToAction("Index", "home");
    }
    else if (result.IsNotAllowed)
    {
        ModelState.AddModelError(string.Empty, _notAllowedLoginMessage);
        return View(model);
    }

    ModelState.AddModelError(string.Empty, _invalidLoginMessage);
    return View(model);
}
```

Code Snippet 4.15: Login action method - *AccountController.cs*

A graphical illustration of the relation between these services and classed can be observed in the class diagram from fig. 4.2.

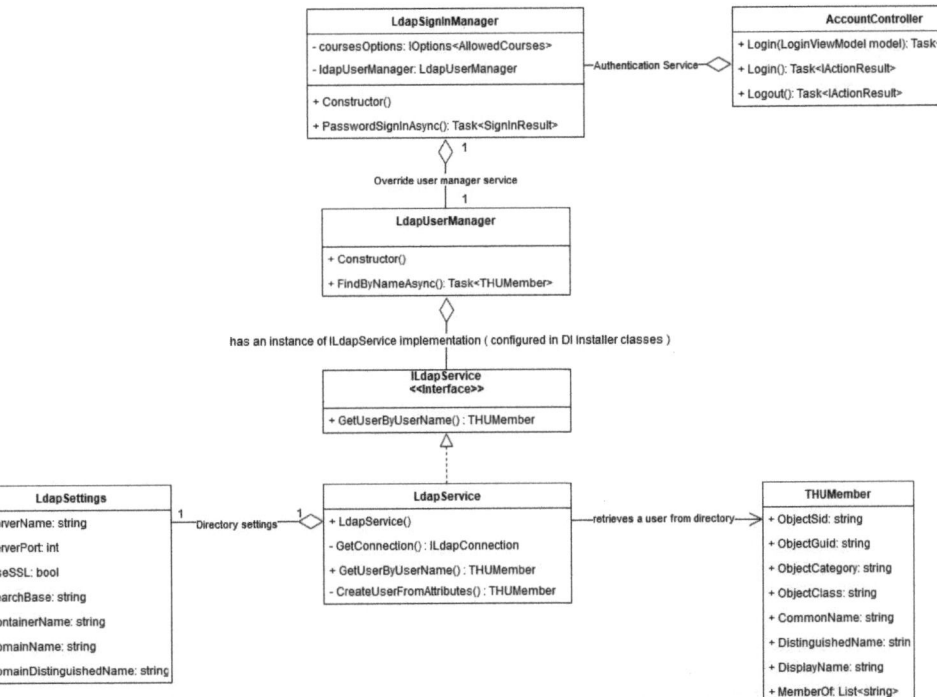

Figure 4.2: Novell's LDAP library implementaion according to Brecht's guide - class diagram

Once, the user logs in, the login action method with the HTTP Post attribute from the "AccountController" is triggered. Thereafter the "PasswordSignInAsync" method of the "LdapSignInManager" service class will be called. Following, the overridden "FindByNameAsync" method from "LdapUserManager" is called which uses the "LdapService" class and forwards the request to the "GetUserByUserName" method, with the user's credentials. This method is binding to the LDAP directory first, with the user's credentials. Upon a successful connection, a connection instance is returned to the caller method. Therefore, on the returned connection instance which is type "ILdapConnection" from the Novell's namespace, the "Search" method is called with the predefined search base, scope, filters, and attributes. The result is passed to the "CreateUserFromAttributes" method, which as the name implies, maps the entity to the "THUMember" business model that represents the user.

Once the "GetUserByUserName" method from "LdapService" returns, in the "SignIn-Methods" the user's courses are compared to the list of mandated courses which are specified in the "appsettings.json" file. If at least one matches, the "SignInManager" validates the request and signs an authentication cookie that is sent to the user. Finally, the user is then redirected to the home page.

4.5 Key Storage Mechanism

Upon successful login, the user is redirected to the home page. A user-friendly dashboard is available, containing basic information, available virtual machine name, the status of the public key as well as the controls over it. A picture of the dashboard can be observed in fig. 4.3.

Figure 4.3: The home page dashboard

As the user is redirected to the home page, the "index" action method from the "HomeController" is triggered. Before the view is displayed, a background script is launched which checks whether the user has already a public key on the target virtual machine. Depending on the application server's operating system, a specific script will be launched. The graphical representation of this mechanism is represented in fig. 4.4.

At runtime, in the "ConfigurationsInstaller" class, depending on the host operating system, a specific implementation will be registered in the DI container for the "IKeyStorageService" interface. In the case of the Linux operating system, "LinuxKeyStorageService" will be configured and the scripts will be loaded from the "BashScripts.json" file, located in the project's "wwwroot/scripts/linux" folder, and bound to the "KeyStorageScripts" class with Options Pattern. The same applies to Windows, except the "WindowsKeyStorageService" class will be registered, and the scripts will be loaded from the "PowerShellScripts.json" file, located in the projects "wwwroot\scripts\windows" folder. The wwwroot folder in ASP.NET is used for storing static files. The "HomeController" has no idea what environment the server is running in, and it communicates with the "IKeyStorageService" interface methods. Thus, the application can be easily migrated from one operating system to another without modifying the code.

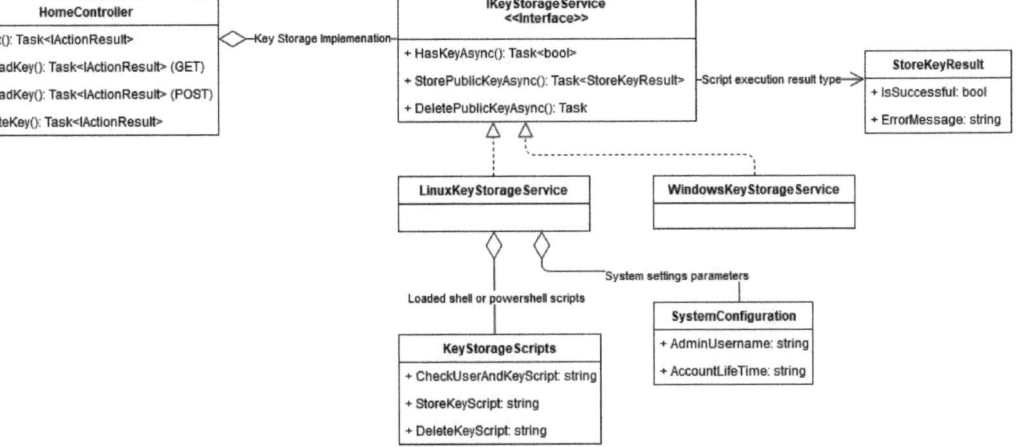

Figure 4.4: Key Storage service - class diagram

4.6 Key Monitoring

Once the user is redirected to "Index" action method from the "HomeController", as explained above, the controller calls the "HasKeyAsync" asynchronous method from the "IKeyStorageService" interface. This method uses the relevant script from the "KeyStorageScript" configuration class, interpolates it with the corresponding values (e.g. user's username, generated account lifetime, etc.). An asynchronous process is started and the output is saved into a string. The script checks first if the account exists on the VM. Thereafter it checks if the user has a local directory and a public key in the ".ssh" folder named "authorized_keys". The script checks every step sequentially, and returns 0 in case of a false assertment. If any zeroes are observed in the process output, means the user has no public key yet and a relevant message is displayed on the dashboard as demonstrated in fig. 4.3. The script can be observed in Code Snippet 4.16

```
grep -c '^{0}:' /etc/passwd;
cd /home;
if [ ! -d \"{0}\" ]; then
    echo 0;
fi;
cd {0};
if [ ! -d \".ssh\" ]; then
    echo 0;
fi;
cd .ssh;
if [ ! -e \"authorized_keys\" ]; then
    echo 0;
fi;
```

Code Snippet 4.16: Key Monitoring shell script

4.7 Key Upload/Update

In order to upload or update the key, the user has to click the upload button on the dashboard. Thereafter he is redirected to the upload key page that is displayed in fig. 4.5.

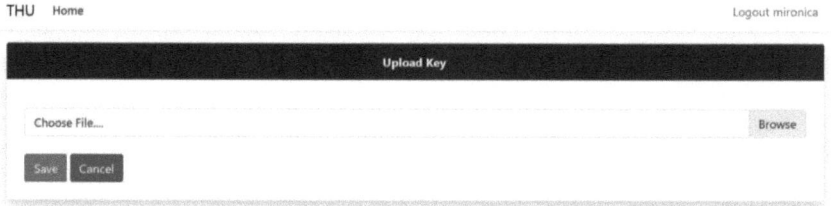

Figure 4.5: The upload key page

The same operation is performed on the server to upload or update key action. When the user selects the key and pushes the save button as shown in fig. 4.5, the

"UploadKey" action method with the HTTP Post attribute is triggered. If the model is valid, which is the uploaded key, the public key is asynchronously stored in the application's "wwwroot/temp-keys" folder, then the "StorePublicKeyAsync" method from the "IKeyStorageService" is called. That will launch the appropriate script from the "KeyStorageScripts" options class. The script contains a few placeholders, and it will be interpolated with the appropriate values. The script for uploading the key is first checking if the users exist, and it will create one with a limited lifetime if it does not exist. The lifetime of the newly generated accounts can be configured from "appsettings.json" file under the "SystemConfiguration" section. The user's directory is therefore protected against any access from other users. In the next step, the ".ssh" folder in the user's directory is created if it does not exist already, and same access rules are applied to it as for the user's directory. Thereafter, regardless of the precedent step, if the ".ssh" folder was created or not, everything inside is deleted. Next, the script will load the public key from the "wwwroot" folder and it will move it to the user's directory on the VM. In order to perform this step, in the "application.json" file under the "SystemConfigurations" section, the application's host username from the VM has to be set. The rights for reading the key are given to the user, and the key is renamed to "authorized_keys".

The script can be observed in Code Snippet 4.17.

```
#!/bin/bash
if [ $(grep -c '^{0}:' /etc/passwd) == 0 ]; then
    sudo useradd -e $(date -d \"{3} days\" +\"%Y-%m-%d\") -m {0};
    sudo chmod 700 /home/{0};
fi;
cd /home/{0};
if [ ! -d \".ssh\" ]; then
    sudo mkdir .ssh;
    sudo chmod 700 /home/{0}/.ssh;
    sudo chown {0}:{0} .ssh;
    cd .ssh;
else
    cd .ssh;
fi
rm -rf /home/{0}/.ssh/*;
cd /home/{2}/SSHConfigurator/SSHConfigurator/wwwroot/temp-keys;
sudo cp {1} /home/{0}/.ssh;
chown {0}:{0} /home/{0}/.ssh;
cd /home/{0}/.ssh;
sudo mv {1} authorized_keys;
sudo chmod 400 authorized_keys;
chown {0}:{0} authorized_keys;
```

Code Snippet 4.17: Upload key shell script

4.8 Key Delete

The delete process is relatively simple. Once the user clicks the delete button, the "DeleteKey" action method from the "HomeController" is triggered, and the script for deleting the key from the key handling service is launched. Regardless, whether the user has a key or not in his directory in the ".ssh" folder, the following script will be executed.

```
rm -rf /home/{0}/.ssh/*;
```

Code Snippet 4.18: Bash script to delete the key from the user's directory

Eventually, the delete button sends an HTTP Post request to the server. If a user misuses this button, the Google's reCaptcha service will consider it as bot activity and the user will be logged out.

5 Security

5.1 Google reCaptcha v3

Considering the fact that SSH CI is a client-server application, it comes with its native vulnerabilities to open redirect, brute-force attacks as well as open gates for automated bot interactions that have to be addressed. The previously enumerated vulnerabilities and the solution for them is discussed in the current and following sub-chapter of this thesis.

As mentioned, Google reCaptcha is a CAPTCHA system. Such a system determines whether the user is a human or an automated bot. The most common form of CAPTCHA is a type of challenge test, like identifying an image or a simple math calculation. They are mainly used in websites for preventing bots from submitting forms, spamming, and registering. As technology becomes more advanced, so do the cyber criminals. Modern bots are leveraging success in solving old CAPTCHA systems like Google reCaptcha v2. Nevertheless, in SSH CI a relatively new CAPTCHA is used that is Google reCaptcha v3. In comparison with the older systems, reCaptcha v3 is transparent for website visitors. It works seamlessly in the background monitoring user's actions. There are no challenges for the user to solve. For each HTTP Post request the user makes, a JavaScript script provided by reCaptcha v3 is executed on the client web-browser that sends a request to reCaptcha server with a site-key and receives a token in response. This token is sent along with the form data that the user submitted to the SSH CI server. The received reCaptcha token is immediately validated by submitting the token with a secret key to a Google reCaptcha validation service. If the token received from the client hasn't tampered, the Google server responds with HTTP 200 and a JSON response. The response contains a property called "Success". It has a score from 0 to 1 that represents how likely is the fact that the request originates from a bot. The lower the score, the higher the probability that the user is a bot. The advantage of reCaptcha v3 over older systems is that specific actions can be defined for each score range. In SSH CI, if the score falls below 0.5 the user is logged out of the system, or his requests are rejected if he tries to log in. In the SSH CI use case, the reCaptcha v3 addresses two threats at the same time, the brute-force attacks during login and bot activity. A graphical demonstration of this process can be observed in fig. 5.1.

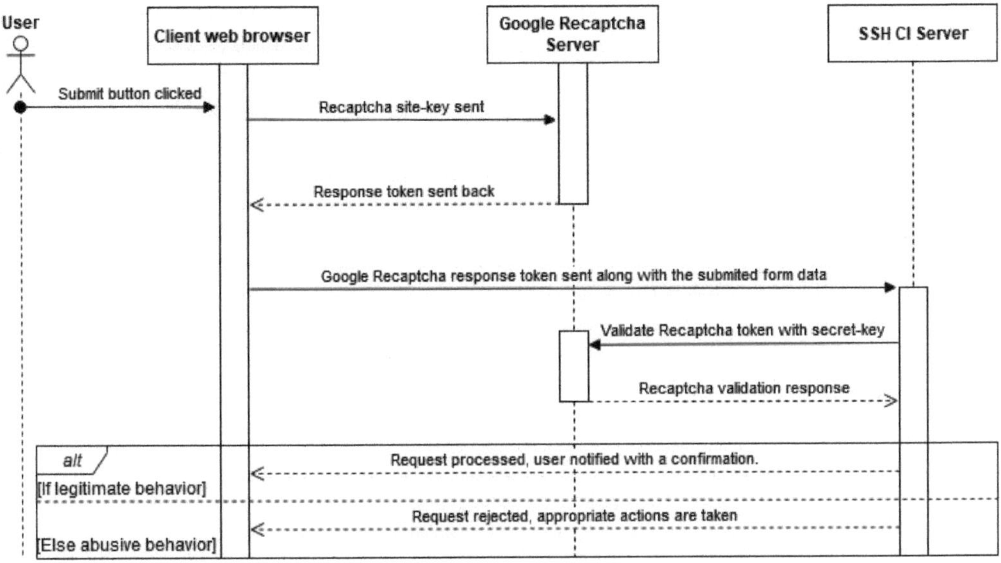

Figure 5.1: Google reCatpcha v3 workflow - sequence diagram

The reCaptcha site-key and secret-key are stored in the "appsettings.json" file. They are bound to a typed class with the Options pattern. Whenever a user requests a web-page protected by reCaptcha, the server selects the appropriate view, injects the site-key in it, and sends it to the client along with the Javascript (JS) script. Implementing reCaptcha v3 in any application is a standardized procedure which is described in the Google reCaptcha's documentation.

5.2 Open-Redirect Attack

Whenever the user accesses any path of SSH CI, the server will either return the desired page or will redirect the user to the login page if a valid authentication cookie was not found in the request header. The originally requested URL will be saved in the query string, and the user will be redirected there after successful login. Such implementation is valuable for the UX, however, it is vulnerable to Open Redirect attacks. This attack is explained with the following example. A malicious user might bait an SSH CI user into clicking a link to the SSH CI login page with a return URL to his twin website's login page at:

`https://www.ssh-ci.de/account/login?returnUrl=https://www.ssh-cl.de/account/login`

The user successfully logs in, the server will parse the returnUrl that is `WWW.SSH-CL`, and will redirect the user to the attacker's page, that looks exactly the same. The user might think the first log in attempt was unsuccessful and will log in again, submitting his credentials to the attacker's server, and thereafter is redirected back to the real website. As result, the user is unaware that his credentials are compromised. Such attack is easily prevented in SSH CI by checking the return URL first with the "LocalRedirect" method provided by ASP.NET Core that ensures that user will be redirected locally within the application. Thus, the possibility of such an attack is reduced to null.

6 Conclusion

This chapter outlines the goals and conclusions of this thesis and how they were accomplished. Furthermore, it emphasizes the weaknesses and strengths of the provided solution. Finally, small guidance for further development of this solution is provided. Sharing a cloud-based virtual machine across many users is a common story line for most of the universities and corporations. As already known from the foundings of this thesis, the problem in this scenario is the amount of maintenance work for system administrators. Given this problem, one fact can be easily deducted. With confidence, it can be said that this is an automation problem. Most of the tasks don't necessitate human touch, hence, delegating them to an automated system is the key to eliminating errors and saving time in the daily business. The SSH CI project is a decent solution to this problem. It is a loosely coupled system that is designed to be modular and extendable. With an improved DI registration mechanism and an interface-based architecture, the application can be used as a reference for similar scale projects. The application is fully documented and follows all the best practices recommended by this thesis. The world's leading cloud platforms like AWS and Microsoft Azure have already implemented analog solutions a long time ago. As proven by their reputation, such setups are performing remarkably. Despite the initial requirement of making an application that would run on Linux, SSH CI is designed to be cross-platform, therefore it can be easily migrated to other operating systems. Nevertheless, SSH CI just like its analog systems has its own pitfalls. Considering it is a client-server application, gaps in the security layer had to be considered. Common vulnerabilities like open redirect, brute-force attacks have been patched, however, as the technology evolves, potential vicious uses cases have to be continuously addressed. A rather small drawback can be considered the maintenance work. However, considering the application is designed with scalability and maintainability in mind, and since the error handling is automated, maintenance is just conditional.

In conclusion, it is crystal clear that the SSH CI is the faultless candidate to the discussed problem. Deducing from the gathered wisdom out of this thesis, in any similar scenario where there is a choice between automating a task or not, the outcome choice should stand for the software side as it's less error-prone and more efficient.

6.1 Discussion

For a small-sized organization, where there is only one available cloud-based virtual machine the provided solution is adequate. However, if there were more virtual machines, the current solution has to support a couple of changes that could be easily implemented. In the current setup, the application is meant to run on the target VM that will be exposed to the users for establishing an SSH session. All the key manipulation scripts are run on the same machine. If control over more virtual machines would be added, the only change would be that the scripts will have to be executed remotely. Both the front-end and the back-end can be easily adapted for that. Considering that the SSH key manipulation logic is implemented in a service that is injected in the controller with the DI, a similar service can be implemented that will mainly use the same scripts. However, an additional module has to be added that will start an SSH session with the target VM first with root access, and then it will execute the existing scripts there. Thus, SSH CI has the full potential of extending and adding more features without having to modify the core architecture.

Another step that can be taken, is strengthening the security layer of the application by further configuring the Google reCaptcha service. For different score ranges, different actions can be taken. For example, if the score falls between 0.2 and 0.5, a Google reCaptcha v2 challenge can be prompted to the user as an additional verification step in case of suspicious activity.

List of Code Snippets

List of Figures

Bibliography

[1] C# Corner Abhishek Yadav. *Middleware*. URL: https://web.archive.org/web/20201010214643/https://www.c-sharpcorner.com/article/asp-net-core-mvc-request-life-cycle/ (visited on October 10, 2020).

[2] Brecht's Blog Brecht Baekelandt. *LDAP Directory Authentication*. URL: https://web.archive.org/web/20201014021907/https://www.brechtbaekelandt.net/blog/post/authenticating-against-active-directory-with-aspnet-core-2-and-managing-users (visited on October 1, 2020).

[3] Microsoft Co. *ASP.NET Core MVC*. URL: https://docs.microsoft.com/en-us/aspnet/core/mvc/overview?view=aspnetcore-3.1 (visited on September 23, 2020).

[4] Microsoft Co. *C#*. URL: https://docs.microsoft.com/en-us/dotnet/csharp/tour-of-csharp/ (visited on September 23, 2020).

[5] Microsoft Co. *Directory Service*. URL: https://docs.microsoft.com/en-us/previous-versions/windows/desktop/ldap/what-is-a-directory-service (visited on October 2, 2020).

[6] Microsoft Co. *Options Pattern*. URL: https://docs.microsoft.com/en-us/aspnet/core/fundamentals/configuration/options?view=aspnetcore-3.1 (visited on October 2, 2020).

[7] Microsoft Co. *Razor*. URL: https://docs.microsoft.com/en-us/aspnet/core/mvc/views/razor?view=aspnetcore-3.1 (visited on September 24, 2020).

[8] Microsoft Co. *System.DirectoryServices Namespace*. URL: https://docs.microsoft.com/en-us/dotnet/api/system.directoryservices? (visited on September 24, 2020).

[9] Mozilla Foundation. *HTTP Cookies*. URL: https://developer.mozilla.org/en-US/docs/Web/HTTP/Cookies (visited on October 2, 2020).

[10] The jQuery Foundation. *jQuery?* URL: https://jquery.com/ (visited on September 24, 2020).

[11] LLC Google. *RECAPTCHA*. URL: https://www.google.com/recaptcha/about/ (visited on September 25, 2020).

[12] SSH Communications Security Inc. *Key Pair - Public and Private*. URL: https://www.ssh.com/ssh/public-key-authentication (visited on September 22, 2020).

[13] Inc. Novell. *Novell.Directory.Ldap.NETStandard*. URL: https://github.com/dsbenghe/Novell.Directory.Ldap.NETStandard (visited on September 24, 2020).

[14] Inc. Wikimedia Foundation. *Bootstrap (front-end framework)*. URL: https://en.wikipedia.org/wiki/Bootstrap_(front-end_framework) (visited on September 24, 2020).

[15] Neil Wilson. *LDAP*. URL: https://ldap.com/license/ (visited on October 2, 2020).